Gleanings *from the* Glenkens

The Glenkens Writers' Group

The Glenkens Writers' Group wish to thank the Glenkens Community and Arts Trust's Connecting in Communities project, funded by the Big Lottery Fund and LEADER, for their support in the production of this publication.

Many thanks to Merryn Fergusson, June Nelson and Ros Elphinstone for their help in preparing the text, and to Martha Schofield, our designer. Thanks also to Mike Brown, who shifted the management of this project from the back of an envelope into the digital age.

Published 2017 by J&B Print, 32A Albert Street, Newton Stewart

ISBN   978-1-9998567-1-7

Compilation © Glenkens Community & Arts Trust
Contributions © individual authors
Graphics © Martha Schofield Design

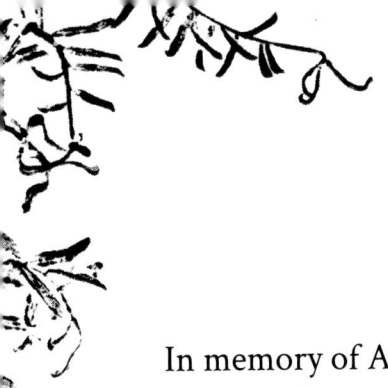

In memory of Anne Mellor and Heather Bradley,
former members of this group.

Preface

This publication celebrates the fourth anniversary of the Glenkens Writers' Group. The group first met in October 2013. We've been joined by new members over the years and, all in all, it has been a remarkably cohesive group.

A lot can happen in four years, in life and in writing. Those brave people who came along initially probably had little idea of what to expect. Some came announcing that they'd never written anything before. Of course that wasn't quite true. Everyone had been writing since primary school: letters, diaries, application forms, work reports, shopping lists and so on. What these self-styled beginners meant was that, although they might have written professionally in one way or another, they hadn't written poetry, fiction or memoir.

Often the most useful aid to a writer is to be given a little time and space dedicated to writing, and the challenge of next month's deadline. Enthusiasm for different genres did vary. Sonnet-writing for instance was enjoyed by some but not all. Sometimes there was mild resistance to a peculiarly perverse homework exercise, but this tenacious group have never been daunted to the point of giving up. They have also encouraged each other in new endeavours and experiments, always giving each other the best kind of support.

It has been a delight to work with such receptive and enthusiastic writers. In editing this volume, I am struck yet again by the dedication each person has shown, in finding the right words, and the right medium, to express what they have to say. The experiences of twelve lives have gone into this book: that's a rich resource in terms of memories, ideas, humour, talent and philosophy. And all in the space of one slim volume.

Margaret Elphinstone

New Galloway, October 2017

CONTENTS

Author	Pages
Stella Cruickshank	7 to 12
Merryn Fergusson	13 to 18
Roger Adams	19 to 24
Ann Maxwell	25 to 27
Margaret Pringle	28 to 33
Wendy Davis	34 to 39
Gordon Hill	40 to 44
Christine Rae	45 to 49
Barry Bryan-Dixon	50 to 54
Carol Salsbury	55 to 60
Philip Hussey	61 to 66
Beverley Vaux	67 to 72
About the contributors	73 to 76

Stella Cruickshank

Crow

The crow came for the child in the night.

Flap, flap, the blue-black wings beat against the pane, a sharp beak pecking at the catch; then under the casement it came and across the sill.

All day the boy had been kicking a ball aimlessly against the back wall of the cottage - thump, thump, thump.

His mother had tried to persuade him to do something else - to read a book, meet his friends - but he ignored her, he was bored. He continued to kick the ball.

So that night the bird took him. Away they flew, over the hills towards where the moon had risen. The boy cried out in fear but the crow replied fiercely, "Do not complain. See how beautiful the sky is: the dark clouds lit by the moon, and the stars above."

All through the night they travelled on. Across the sea, over mountains. Gradually the land below changed from fertile grassland to desert plains. The towns and cities with their pitched roofs and towering spires were replaced by flat-roofed buildings shrouded in clouds of dust.

As the boy peered down he saw that all the buildings were crushed, walls had been ripped revealing the insides of the rooms, with tables set for a meal and beds left as if the people had just risen from sleep; but there was no one.

The boy heard the distant sound of an explosion. Then through the dust clouds a great warplane appeared. The crow dived downwards (to avoid the aeroplane). The boy clung desperately to the bird; then through the dust he saw children playing football amongst the ruins. Another explosion - the children scattered. The crow showed the boy one child left behind. He was curled up amongst rubble, a deep wound in his side, his hands and feet bloodied.

The boy's selfish heart changed, his tears began to flow. On and on they flowed, washing the wound in the child's side and cleaning the blood from his hands and feet.

Eventually the crow turned and flew back in the direction they had come. After many days and many nights he set the boy down upon a rock by the loch of his island home.

His mother had been desperate in her grief when she found her son had gone. She wandered, desolate, across the fields and along the shore. Late one autumn day she saw the old crow upon the gatepost. He flapped up into the air at her approach, and flying ahead, led the woman to her child. She ran to the boy and enfolded him in her arms.

When the boy returned to school, the form mistress told the class that new families had arrived on the island, from a land torn apart by war. She said they should be made welcome. The boy looked across to the newcomer. His skin was brown as tree bark, his hair dark as night, and his hands, resting gently on the desk, bore deep crimson scars.

The Book Festival

"What is it you're doing?"
I enquired of the old man brushing the path.
"I'm sweeping up all the words they left behind.
So many words.
Each year it's the same.
I find them piled in corners;
In the flower beds;
And the wind catches them:
They get blown up
And tossed about:
Ideas get caught in the branches."
"But why so many left behind?"
"O people just throw them about;
So careless."
He fills the sack in his barrow.
"But what is this?
Why is this path clear?
No waste here -
Not a spare word."
"This is where the poets met."
He replied.

Cake

Your pastry lies between us
Untouched.
The crumbs of our conversation
Are scattered on the table,
Until you rise to go,
Carelessly
Brushing our words
To the ground
And with your shoe,
Crush them.

How Can I Convince You?

I'll lay the argument out
Pressed flat beneath my hand
Until, as fine lace,
It's crimped and goffered.

Or should I hang it
Upon the line
To be aired?
No, you will gather it up,
Folding it neatly,
And place it in the back
Of a drawer
To be forgotten.

Future Perfect

I'll be the rabbit with wings.
I'll not play golf in the afternoon,
Or sing in church, though I'm out of tune.
I won't ignore people who 'aren't like us',
Or think it common to catch a bus.
Or have 'drinks', with sherry at six,
And speak, very loudly, of 'social mix'.
I won't wear a blazer or sensible shoes.
I'll listen to jazz and American blues.
I'll read Hegel and Camus and Sartre,
I'll visit the Bauhaus amd praise modern art.
Yes, I'll be the rabbit with wings.

The Plum

The child shares
the ripe plum
with a crow
holding the fruit
cupped in his small hands
while the bird
sinks its great
blue-black beak
into the fruit.

Stella Cruickshank

Shadows

I sit
in the shadows
of the ash tree

my child sleeps
in the shade
of the verandah

while the dog
dozes
on the step

the thin girl
skips
in the sun

the wolf
stares out
from the forest

Merryn Fergusson

Old Father Trump

"You are old Donald Trump," the young man said,
"And your hair is a mad shade of gold.
You started with millions and millions you made
And not all of them legal we're told."

"In my youth," Donald Trump then replied to the boy,
"I feared I might injure or maim,
But bully boy tactics became the best ploy
Why I bulldozed again and again."

"You are old," said the youth "in case you forgot,
You seem to confuse every fact.
Yet you traverse the world and change not one jot.
Pray what is the reason for that?"

"In my youth," said the rogue, his gold locks to the fore,
"I kept all my brain cells so supple
By playing in golf clubs - I own two or more
Allow me to sell you a couple."

Merryn Fergusson

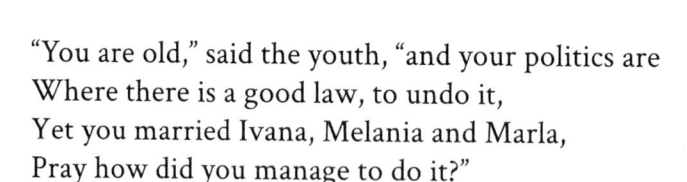

"You are old," said the youth, "and your politics are
Where there is a good law, to undo it,
Yet you married Ivana, Melania and Marla,
Pray how did you manage to do it?"

"In my youth," said his elder, "I lived the high life
And fathered five children, no more,
And the millions I earned I paid out to each wife.
Melania's the one I adore."

"You are old," said the youth, "one would hardly dare hope
That you'd risk shaking hands with another,*
Yet you won an election, and never used dope,
What made you so awfully clever?"

"I can't answer questions I don't understand,"
Said Trump senior, "So remove that damned mike!
I'm President-elect of America's land,
You're fired! And I'll do as I like!"

* *Trump is a germaphobe, hates shaking hands,
has never drunk or done drugs.*

The Suitcase

"Your game is up, my lass!"

That is what my Aunt said to me when she sent me up here. She said to go to my room but if I hide here at the top of the stairs I can see what is happening.

Aunt is talking outside on the front doorstep to the lady from the Social. She does that, talks outside, when she does not want us to hear what they are saying. We were meant to be in the living room, with Pixie. Pixie is wearing her school clothes, although it is the holidays. When they started playing 'rock-paper-scissors' I couldn't play because five was too many, so I went to the kitchen.

I had seen where my Aunt had hidden her trinket box. It was on the top shelf of the cupboard. I pulled a chair across from the table. Standing on the counter, I could just reach. I only took out the necklace. It had a pink stone which was easy to break off when I bashed it with the poker from the range. I went out to where my Aunt was talking and held out my hand to show her the necklace. "Look what Pixie has done now!" I said.

She didn't answer like she usually does, but looked a bit queer. "Excuse me," she said to the woman and she held my shoulder quite tight and took me back to the kitchen. That's when she said, "Your game is up, my lass". She pulled the chair from the counter and pushed it back under the table. "Go to your room."

Pixie came here last summer just before we went back to school. She's been here a whole year. They, my family, really like Pixie which means that they might not like me. She went into Primary two. I was in Primary two when I came here. Hector is in Primary four, I am in Primary five, and Eddie is in Primary seven. Clifford goes to the big school. My brothers are not my real brothers.

It is a long walk to school so Eddie gives Pixie a piggy-back, especially on the way back when we get to the stony road. Eddie always looks after Pixie. He's tough on her too. When she wouldn't learn her two-times tables he lifted her up in the air and said he would drop her if she didn't say them. So she did. He knew she could.

Hector and I usually get sent to our room when we are bad, or are made to clean out the hens, or bring in the logs, but I don't mind. There are twenty-two steps up the stairs and I know the ones that sound creaky, but it didn't matter. Not today. Clifford can slide the whole way down the bannisters. Eddie tried but he fell, not badly. We are not allowed to slide down the bannisters but Clifford sometimes holds Pixie and slides from halfway. I can do from halfway on my own. When I sit here I can feel around the railings and go round the bends and bumps. I can pick at the paint and flick it off. It would be better if I could use my nails, but I bite them. Now Aunt and the lady from the Social are in the kitchen. Pixie's suitcase is at the bottom of the stairs. The others are playing 'my grandmother's cat'.

Before Pixie came to stay with us my Aunt said that I had to go with her to a meeting. "We have to go so that you can stay with us," Aunt said. Aunt is not my real Aunt. The trouble is, my Mum can't look after me. I like living with my Aunt and my Dad. I call him Dad because I don't have one. Then Aunt told all of us that at the meeting they would decide if my little sister can stay here too. I didn't know that I had a little sister but that sounded nice.

There were a lot of people in the meeting room but I could sit close to my Aunt. If I leant forward I could see my sister. A woman who I thought I knew was holding her hand but she looked messy, not tidy like everyone else. I was wearing my school clothes. That messy lady got very upset during the meeting. She pointed at me and said, "You can have that one! Get her out of my sight!" Everyone in the room started moving and speaking, but then it calmed down. The next day Pixie came to live with us.

I don't know when it started. I think it was when I dared Pixie to jump off the mantelpiece onto the sofa. Eddie and Clifford can do it and land on the floor. I pushed her and her foot hit the glass ornament. It made a big crash and my Aunt came in. Pixie was holding a piece of the broken glass. I stepped away nearer the curtains. "What's this?" My Aunt stood in front of Pixie, but Pixie could see me. I fixed her with my eyes. "You dare clipe," I was trying to say.

"Did you do this?" Pixie was looking at me and then she looked down and nodded her head.

Aunt was not cross with her. She spoke gently. She said that little girls were not supposed to break things, but it was all right because they would not send her away.

When it happened again, after the window got broken, Aunt said that I was to go alone with her to collect the eggs. I was allowed to reach into the nesting boxes and pass the eggs carefully to Aunt who put them in her basket. Aunt told me that I would need to help Pixie and that we had to stop her from destroying things. She said that Pixie was testing us out, to see if we really wanted her. She said that I could let her know when things got broken.

My Dad has some stuffed animals and birds on the landing, and the owl's case broke. Hector told Pixie that she was silly to own up to something that she hadn't done. I made sure that he wasn't around after that when things got broken.

This morning Aunt and I packed Pixie's suitcase. I collected her clothes, the toys that she likes and her favourite book. Aunt said, "Where is Squirrel?" I knew that Pixie kept it under her pillow. We don't have teddies or soft toys but Eddie bought Squirrel at the school sales table, and she always sleeps with it. "Well done!" Aunt said. "Do you remember what a scrawny waif you were when you arrived? You ran away that first day because you were frightened of the goats, and you ran all the way to the other side of the village." Aunt sometimes tells this story. The policeman brought me back in his car. Aunt always laughs. "What a joke! The man whose children make the most trouble in the village was the one who picked you up and took you to the police station."

My knees are sore. I think that I will get my pillow. They are walking around downstairs so they won't hear me. That's better! I can still see if I put my pillow against the wall. When I looked out of my window I saw that the lady from the Social has gone because her car is not where she parked it.

It was not too bad when things got broken like Hector's Action Man. Clifford and Eddie made a new game where the Action Man was wounded and they rescued him from our bedroom window. It was after Aunt's mirror got cracked, the one she has by her hairbrush, that things changed. I heard her and my Dad talking. They said that having Pixie was not working and that they would have to send her back.

I wanted it to stop. The breaking and the telling, but I liked it when Aunt was happy with me. She didn't shout and say 'I don't like that one' about Pixie, but I could tell what they were planning. Then our Dad told us that they had rung the Social and Pixie was going to another family.

I think Aunt is in the living room. They were playing I-spy. They have shut the door again.

It is getting boring, waiting.

The suitcase is still there.

Someone's opened the door.

Hector is running and coming up the stairs. I'll stay here and then he'll see me.

"Pixie is staying!" He was puffed and then he said it again. "Pixie is staying! She didn't break everything after all, it was you, you wanted her sent away...." He went like this, and put his hand over his mouth. "I am not allowed to say." Then he went to the bathroom.

The lady from the Social didn't take Pixie away.

And she didn't take me away either.

Roger Adams

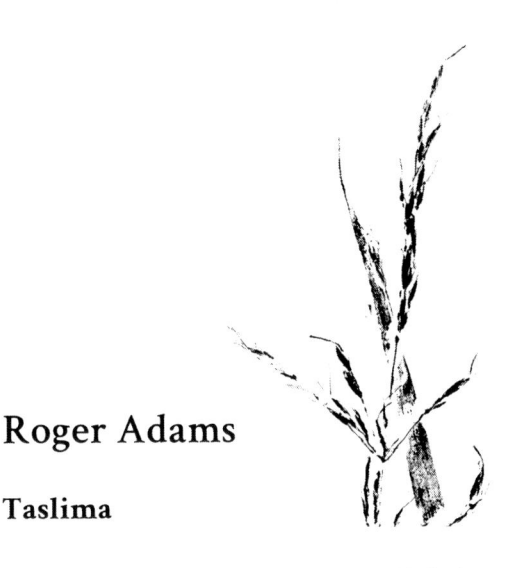

Taslima

In Bangladesh a storm has collided with tidal bores and together they have razed huts and villages, washing the people away. Briefly this becomes news. Listening to the usual BBC suspects I always think how soon, safely flying BA, they will 'lift off' after a 'quick change', to return to the UK, appropriately clothed.

What if their world was turned upside down? What if one day an anonymous survivor, blown ashore, and found in a refugee camp, after losing all her family one awful night, was to become the local BBC correspondent and presenter? A character shaped by adversity. I have a candidate in mind. I was helped to success in my project relief work, 2002/4, by a survivor. She was Taslima, an outstanding young woman Field Worker for the Hardcore Poor.

For capacity and for intelligence, for a preparedness to learn, she was head and shoulders above the male Project Officers.

1996, Taslima, aged fourteen, had wandered on the shore among the wrecked bodies of women, men and children. Found her family dead among the carcasses of cows and calves, after the storm. Remained on the beach, attracting little attention. Shivering and weeping, she chose to survive, cooking a dead fish that she had recovered. It was food for her and three small children, gathered to her.

Taslima, destitute, was lucky: she became one more servant in a rich family's household. She had left-over food to eat and her kitchen sleeping space. Families who possess cars drive down to the beaches in the aftermath of a flood. They click their cameras so they can return to Dhaka with dramatic photographs and replacement servants. Why not, if possessed of a huge place in exclusive Dhamondi? I always noticed in the bigger houses I visited, the many harried young servant girls, always head-down with tasks and if not working then sleeping. "Oh!" my host commented, answering my question, "We don't notice them." He smiled at me, amidst laughter.

Taslima progressed. When I met her she was a project Field Worker, 22 years old, still unmarried. She was extraordinary, the stand-out personality amongst the young women Field Workers of my project. She had won her promotion as reward for never being overlooked! She had taught herself English, enough to communicate with me whilst her compatriots just stared, speaking only Bangla. She wittily answered the men back, displaying confident assertion, hinting at contempt. Where she sat, prominent in the front row amongst the women, much laughter originated. I was sometimes the cause. Her face was expressive, memorable. Her impact on me was strong enough for me to want to write about her. I can visualise her, medium height, always in a tatty green salwar. Without her participation in my survey of the Hard Core Poor (the typical question 'have you had a little rice in the past three days?'), in the twelve villages, the Oxfam-funded project would not have been accurately completed.

Taslima cheerfully entered my life by walking into my bungalow and greeting me: "Mr Rozar", while others kept a distance, no intrusion. Almost unaware, she became my lieutenant. One hot June day I rode my black heavy Chinese bike along a dirt path above paddy fields toward a village, hopeful of completing day one of my survey of village women Hard Core Poor. I would share most of the work with Taslima. Ahead through the mango trees there she was, at the centre of a circle of sixty village women amongst whom sat blank-eyed young girls, married, pregnant. Her understanding of the survey process was unrivalled. Over three months, we completed the work together.

Six in the morning, my farewell to Pradrishapur and, now used to rickshaw sway and bump, I looked around with mixed feelings. Once past our offices a young Muslim woman's figure and face emerged from the shadow.

"Goodbye Mr Rojar. Goodbye and thank you, thank you!"

Inside The Call Box

Standing, standing, standing is my only choice. I can feel my body is having a 'hate on' against the absolute tedium of the four close surrounding walls. Oh this red-painted numerous small-windowed box designed for confinement and built to prevent breaking out other than by use of the door. 16-year-old male bodies like mine like to get ready for action.

Mine is now actively rotating side to side as I grow more impatient with waiting, waiting, waiting. Soon muscle cramp will hit and I will curse my fate. This is trial by apparently being sentenced to open-ended call-box misery. Kafka should have written about callbox suffering at the hands of women, those who entice men into call-boxes with hopes and fantasy and vivid anticipation. This can get such a hold on a man's reason, imagining and expecting, not yet boasting of success, but now hoping 'that' is what might happen soon, compelling him to remain lodged like a vagrant in this very confined space. I mean what sort of success is call-box frustration? It's hope kept alive by telephone silence. Choices. Well the first and only choice is yet again to indulge in fidgeting, turning about in this small space. I raise my knee against the door for the change of it being open half an inch for one half minute.

I smile at a grandma outside waiting on me, smile some more, but am not leaving. WHY? Because 'I'm waiting for her call to come in' of course. This is as it is in the Joan Baez song that I cannot, not be not, not be listening to on my tape head set. I keep sane by listening to best tracks of choice 1980s music for great... Oh my imagination, listening as if her lover. Yep, in this booth, life means nothing expected ever happens, nothing as hoped for by me. The black phone set is provocatively silent, just in its place, solid and quite pointless as an object when not doing its stuff. I give her more time to ring so the world can be told how I kept my word. I know women are the devil, handing out call-box imprisonment. Look at the sky, no change in colour, at the grass outside, still green, parked car has not moved. I look again at my watch as if for help, then retrieve her letter from my pocket, read again about the time of her call and number. I am now past the tenth reading of it. Then, yes then, then, the phone rings and exactly on time grandma outside opens my phone box door and reaching for my phone says,

"It will be for me".

Time's Beautiful Mice

One night, now a year ago, Helen finds memory too strong for sleep on this, her first night as a widow. Her bedroom light is on, illuminating, at 3 am, her stairs, for descent. She decides to begin assembling an archive, searching for an answer to a question, 'who had her husband been before he became a monster?'

She finds and opens his diaries, looks at his early writing, searches for lost identity. She was thankful at his death as they all had been. She had hoped for it with hate and loathing for the man monster they had to endure for decades, once his diagnosis had been confirmed.

She opens his diary: after they met in 1970 she finds he is practising his writing style and describing what he remembered about their meeting.

Tottenham Court Road, a slow perambulation down today, evening, drenching rain turning to snow. I shiver, enjoy revisiting the step in the dark waiting for her, perhaps she will awaken desire in me, like the first time.

About that January rendezvous, in the year 1970, he'd added: *I believed in a few minutes this one evening, I can change my life.*

He noted: *We hurried into a cab, sometime before midnight, out of the cold January night.*

Other diaries she opens, scanning for entries, summoning memory, recall. More than anything she wants to know how he wrote about their marriage and the events which followed. She scans the pages for 1972, the year their first child was born, a boy. She begins a search of entries, anticipating his words about when their baby needed changing after his Polio inoculation and how it fatefully fell to him to contract Polio from the small cut on his thumb.

Wistfully she imagines occasional happy diary entries, reminders of the witty, flamboyant musician, poet and writer who, at eighteen, could choose between a prestigious School of Music and Sussex University.

Next day, on her return home from a walk she finds, as if a voice from another time, one of the friends from his youth who had been at the funeral.

Not pleased, she admits this friend into her kitchen. Unwanted, yet quite determined that he should talk well of his old friend, he had dropped by, not by arrangement, but because her husband was, he claims, the most remarkable man he had ever met. So he had come to pay his respects. He wanted to remember, to be wishing old times back.

She has to hear him out, feels challenged. The dead husband becomes almost present in the room. She hears again the jokes - his jokes - and that voice. The visitor is visibly delighted to achieve his re-enchantment of the past, bringing forth laughter from her.

Later, much later, the widow goes to her room knowing that her huge relief at his death has been replaced by grief. She understands the cruelty of time, how in a minute a life can change forever and the consequences become a ripple connecting past with present times.

Ann Maxwell

Winter Still

A leaden sky sifts snow, flakes fall, so white
It blots all colour from the countryside,
To leave a strange new world of monochrome
And silence; as if it holds its breath and waits.

No wisp of air disturbs this magic cloak
As ice mascara deftly frosts each twig.
The feather touch of flakes upon your head;
Thick powder snow that creaks beneath your boots;
Just deep impressions where your feet have trod
Record the only sign of life that's passed.

Next dawn, one ray of sun lit up the tops
Of trees, and flushed them with a coat of rose.
A surge of joy for anyone who'd seen
Before a cloud snuffed out the truant beam.

Past, Present and Future

Had set out with a purpose
Am distracted on the way
Now, whatever was that purpose?

Autumn

The tree stands, weary from its summer show.
Leaves hang, and smoulder to a golden hue.
The sun highlights their richly painted glow
Until a thieving wind purloins a few.
Then stabbing frost, and biting breezes snatch
A fluttering fall of amber, red, and brown
Which children chase, and jump and try to catch
One airborne leaf, before it touches down.
This leaf, whatever colour, shape, or size
Has power to grant a month of happiness,
And so, borne home in triumph as a prize.
But all remaining left as valueless
Their winter work, with worms deep in the earth
Recycles leaves to fuel the tree's rebirth.

An Encounter

We used to ride along the forest tracks hopeful of seeing abundant wildlife there, but the woods were strangely silent, apart from the buzzing cloud of flies over each head. Cantering on to escape them gave a moment's relief, but on slowing down they instantly re-formed.

One day, walking there alone, no horse or dog, and thoughts roaming like shadows of windblown clouds, something drew my eyes a little way ahead to a clearing, and there, a stag stood watching me. I paused, and stopped, amazed and wondering how long he had been observing me. What was he thinking?

As I returned his gaze I felt I'd stumbled into his world and owed him an apology. We studied each other, and then, as though accepting me, with total lack of haste, his head relaxed, he gently moved away and melted back into the trees and was gone.

In those moments we seemed to share each other's lives, and then undisturbed go on our separate ways.

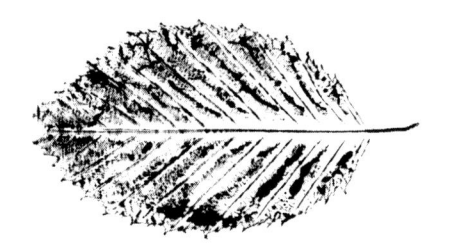

Margaret Pringle

Tanganyika 1956

After three weeks at sea the ship sailed slowly into the harbour at Dar-es-Salaam. The name means 'Haven of Peace' and it lived up to its name; white sand, palm trees, and old buildings, hot under a tropical sun. Everyone on board, civil servants returning from home leave, seemed familiar with the procedure of leaving the ship in order to proceed up-country by train to their various postings. Everyone, that is, except me! One of my trunks was missing, and while they were looking for it I was becoming worried that I would miss the train. However I was assured that it would not go without me, and sure enough, there it stood, patiently hissing steam until my errant luggage was found and put on board followed by its relieved owner. Ah well, this was Africa after all! I was glad to be shown to my compartment and after the evening meal settled into my bunk and soon fell asleep.

I woke early to find everything, including my face, covered in fine red dust. By the time I had washed my face in the tiny washbasin the train was slowing down, and with a lot of hissing of steam and loud rattling it came to a stop opposite a sign saying 'Moshi' - my destination. The guard came bustling along the train to tell me that my luggage was on the platform, so down I stepped to be transfixed by the sight of the snow-covered summit of Kilimanjaro, which seemed to soar above me in the intense blue sky. A few people got off the train and disappeared through the small dusty station, leaving me alone on the platform with my two rather battered-looking trunks and the station master. As instructed I had sent a telegram from Dar-es-Salaam to the Agricultural Officer - the 'A.O.' - in Moshi informing him of my arrival, but there was no-one to meet me.

The station master suggested that I leave my luggage with him to be picked up later, and walk a few hundred yards up the road to have breakfast at the hotel. I entered the hotel which was relatively cool and dark compared with the blinding sunlight outside. An African wearing a kanzu (a long white robe) and red fez appeared out of the shadows, salaamed, and asked if I would like to sit. Feeling rather relieved that he spoke English, I said that I would like breakfast, whereupon he showed me to a table and recited what food was available. I settled for ham and eggs and toast and marmalade.

He disappeared quietly, leaving me to take in my surroundings. The heavy wooden furniture looked a bit shabby and very dusty. He reappeared with plates which he carefully polished on the sleeve of his kanzu before laying them on the table. I'm sure my eyebrows must have shot up, but I had more on my mind than hygiene at that moment.

Breakfast duly arrived, the smell of bacon making me realise how hungry I was, and I ate with enjoyment. I again asked where I would find the office of the A.O. and was directed up the hill to the 'boma'. This was reassuring but at the same time rather puzzling, as a boma, which I recollected from reading fiction, was an enclosure surrounded by thorn branches to keep livestock safe from predators. This quiet little town didn't actually look like the sort of place where lions would be wandering around at night, but who knows.

I walked up the hill and came to a collection of single storey buildings arranged in a rectangle and a sign indicating the offices of the Department of Agriculture. I introduced myself to the clerk in the first office. He took me to meet Ian Constantinesco, the A.O. who shook hands and asked why I had not sent a telegram. I replied that I had done so, whereupon he smiled apologetically and said that he hadn't received it yet. Anyhow, over a cup of coffee he arranged for my luggage to be delivered to my bungalow, and took me to see my new abode. It stood in a street close to the boma under tall shady trees, and was relatively cool. My two trunks, containing all my worldly goods, had already arrived, and the A.O. suggested that I settle in. He would call back in the early evening and take me to meet his wife and have dinner with them.

The bungalow contained all the basic furniture necessary, including a paraffin-fuelled refrigerator, but was very Spartan and drab, although comfortable enough.

I had just started to unpack when a cheery chap arrived and informed me that I was his replacement, and that he would be leaving in a few days' time. With him was a small wiry African whom he introduced as 'Safari', his 'boy', and asked if I would like to take him over as my servant. It hadn't occurred to me that I would need a servant but, as he pointed out, the domestic facilities were so basic that everyone employed a house 'boy' to collect wood for the kitchen stove and to heat the water; to cook in the lean-to kitchen at the back of the house, to clean and do the 'dhobi' - the washing and ironing. He added that Safari wasn't a first-class house boy but he would be very useful to take with me on safari, and besides, he needed a job. I realised that my first priority would have to be to learn to speak Kiswahili.

After having my employment contract confirmed by the Crown Agents for the Colonies in London, I had been advised to buy the necessary kitchen equipment from a UK company which specialised in this service, and a large crate had already been delivered. Unpacking all this felt a bit like Christmas, although the only luxury that I had allowed myself was a large Thermos flask.

Next morning the Field Officer, David Goode, arrived saying

he had been detailed to get me organised and show me around. First thing was to go down town and open a bank account; then down towards the station to find an Indian tailor to make me some working clothes. I decided on three bush jackets, two pairs of slacks and a skirt and to my surprise was told that one set would be ready for me to pick up the next day. Another 'duka' - or shop - was awash with colour and I chose some really bright furnishing material to be made into curtains and loose covers for the chair cushions. Within a few days the curtains were hung and the cushion covers were in place – a welcome change from the drab khaki cushions, and the place was beginning to feel like a home. There was even a resident black cat whose name was 'Paka'. As I acquired a knowledge of Kiswahili, I learnt that 'paka' simply meant cat, but 'Paka' he remained.

I had assumed that I would be provided with transport, and was somewhat surprised to be told that I would have to provide my own. On pointing out that I had no funds available, I was informed that a government loan would automatically be made available to me and repayment would be deducted from my salary over the period of my three-year contract. Civil servants had to keep a log book of the mileage they travelled and were paid an allowance accordingly each month.

David made some enquiries and took me to have a look at a second hand Peugeot station wagon which he said handled better than most on the muddy roads during the rains. It belonged to a Pole who manufactured sweets and drove around the country selling them to the African dukas. The vehicle looked a bit the worse for wear, but David reckoned that the engine seemed all right, so I crossed my fingers and bought it. As it turned out it did me very well and never broke down on me on the road.

Ian, the A.O., said he didn't quite know what he was expected to do with me. He decided that David Goode could take me around for a couple of weeks to get to know my way around the mountain, and become familiar to the African farmers. After that I would have to find out what I could do to improve the animal husbandry, and make the job my own. This suited me very well as I liked working on my own initiative and enjoyed a challenge.

As I travelled around the mountain roads with David, I very soon noticed the African women, usually in groups of three, walking upwards carrying huge bundles of grass and vegetation on their heads. David told me that each family had a 'shamba' (small farm) of about three acres and there simply wasn't space to graze cattle or grow feed for them. The cattle were stall-fed, and the few goats and fat-tailed sheep were herded by small boys to forage wherever they could. The women understood the value of milk in the diet of small children, which was their reason for keeping cattle. What a burden! It took two people to lift the bundle of heavy fresh cut grass on to the head of the woman carrying it, and she would carry it for hours from the plains below.

However the Wachagga were more fortunate than most in that they were able to grow a valuable cash crop - Arabica coffee - and it was provided with shade by bananas which were the staple food crop. The volcanic soil was very fertile, and the long and short rains gave them a relatively long growing season. They also had an amazingly efficient and widespread system of furrows which had been put in place by the Germans. Tanganyika had been the German colony of German East Africa.

The Department of Agriculture's work on soil conservation was obviously very successful as the slopes were well contoured and there was very little sign of erosion.

At my interview in London, I had been told that the African women tended the livestock but would not approach white men for advice. My employment would be an experiment to establish whether I could make contact and help to improve the standard of animal husbandry on the lower slopes of Kilimanjaro.

It transpired that a previous veterinary officer had established a small patch of possible fodder crops, which I could use to propagate more planting material. This was what I had been hoping to find

- a forage plant that could be grown on the only available space on the shambas, either on the contour banks or along the banks of the water furrows. I chose a bulky palatable-looking grass which obviously thrived and was fast growing where it had a good water supply, and it was relished by the cattle. It would be ideal to grow on the banks of the water furrows. We split up and planted out all the available plants. My next task was to get to know the locals and persuade them to accept my plan.

I enlisted the help of Hippolyte, the local agricultural instructor. He was a dignified elderly man whose lined face was full of character, and he was greatly respected by the people in his area. We set about finding farmers who were willing to cooperate, and in due course supplied them with young grass plants. One had to convince the menfolk first, but the women were quick to realise the benefit of growing fodder on the shambas - a practical approach to a problem.

The cattle, having been kept inside for many generations, and stall fed were very small and low in productivity. A few farmers had Zebu cross Ayrshire cows and they were much more productive enabling their owners to sell milk.

We had some success, but change is very slow in rural Africa. Years later, and thousands of miles from Tanzania - as it was by then known - I picked up a *Time* magazine in a dentist's waiting room. In it was an article entitled: 'President Julius Nyerere visits the grass planting schemes of Kilimanjaro'.

Wendy Davis

Conkers

Russet coloured fingers gently drifting down
A windblown carpet sheltering spheres of treasure
Waiting
Small figures alive with excitement
Crunching leaves underfoot
Searching
Little hands grubbing gleaming gems from hiding,
Polished and cuddled in warm palms, carried home,
Pierced by a skewer, suspended by a string, battered
Which one the conqueror?
Swept aside for soup, sandwiches and the midday news
Abandoned
Forgotten

Drifting windblown sand disguising globes of destruction
Waiting
Hungry faces fearfully navigating the terrain
Searching
Pressure of feet, exploding death
Blood spattered like jewels gleaming
Loved bodies, cradled close, carried home
Swept aside by angry men
Raped, beaten, discarded, conquered
No help
No news
Abandoned
Forgotten

The Climb

It is a long steep walk in. We look down at the cars crawling along the road below and across to the layers of mountain beyond.

Sweating, we sort out our gear, concentrating now on the rock face and the ridge above.

It is a three-pitch climb, classified as 'severe' with a bad step on the second, that I am leading. There is a feeling of anticipation, excitement and a flutter of nerves.

My companion starts to climb. He is strong, skilled and smoothly moves upwards. The sound of hammer on piton comes from the small ledge above. The belay is in place.

"Below."

"Ready to climb?"

"OK."

"Climbing."

High on adrenaline I join him, clip into a krab, and rope-up. It is my turn. Fingers and feet firmly attached, searching for a hold, always with three fixed points, body away from the wall, looking and planning the route ahead. A slow, steady ascent, a short traverse to the left, then up again.

I can't find the next hold.

I'm stuck.

Where to go?

Muscles won't grip for long. If I peel off there is no rope to save me. This is exposed free climbing.

A flash of panic. Control it and think.

Take a calculated risk?

Decision time.

Go.

We complete the climb, sit on the ledge, legs dangling, for a celebratory smoke. Young, relaxed and feeling immortal. Laughing, we scramble to the ridge, sashay along it then speed to the inn below.

It is noisy with released tension and the instant camaradrie of climbers. We squeeze in and add to the chatter.

Later, cocooned in down, rain a rhythmic lullaby on the tent roof, we sleep.

Tomorrow: work, responsibility and different challenges.

The Lane - 1940

The clatter of wheels and horses' hooves came bumping up the lane.

It was the daily signal. Mum took off her pinny, put on her hat and picked up the jugs and money that were always ready on the kitchen table. I collected the tiddy jug for my gill and the carrot tops for Flossie.

"Good morning Mr Moss."

"Good morning Mrs Parker."

"Good morning Mrs Wastell."

It was the morning routine.

The trap had a churn on the back with different sized ladles hooked round the rim to measure the milk. Flossie knew where to stop.

"Morning Ted"

"Morning ladies. The usual?"

"The news is bad again"

The wireless was always switched on, everyone was anxious for the latest war report.

The milk was doled out. "Git up." Ted and Flossie moved on.

The ladies settle down for their morning crack.

"Mrs Stokes is beside herself. Walter is at Dunkirk and there is no news of him. Poor soul doesn't know where to turn."

"Gordon is being sent overseas. They told him yesterday. Mrs Richardson is worried sick. He is no'but a lad."
"Have you heard Lil is getting married? Mrs Green has got hold of some parachute silk for the dress."
"That will cost her coupons."
"Well, farmers have ways and means. When is it?"
"Next month."
"That's quick."
"She'll soon be starting to show."
"Shhh." Mum looks at me. "Little pigs have big ears. Did you hear ITMA last night?" She changes the subject.

All the lane was invited to the wedding.

Everyone was looking forward to it, then Maurice Baines brought mumps home from school and we were all quarantined.

On the day, Mrs Baines was put in charge of us. We were all cleaned up and lined up on the front lawn to watch. The adults went first, walking down the lane to the trolley bus, all dressed up in their baggy pre-war best. After a while a black car came bouncing along with Farmer Green and Lil in her white dress, smiling and waving. It was soon past.

We thought it was all a big fuss but we didn't appreciate it was a small spot of sunshine in those dark depressing days.

Backfire

The first day of April; spring is here, the sky is blue, it's Saturday morning so no alarm. Simon is already showered and dressed. The cat who doesn't recognise weekends has long departed.
"Time to get moving. Mrs B will be here with her vacuum any time now."
"Kids are quiet, wonder what they're up to?"
"There was a lot of rushing about earlier."
Suddenly, screams. We dash downstairs: Mrs B is pale and shaking. The boys, horrified, flee upstairs.
"There's a body in the study - dead!"
We stand for a moment, frozen.
"Call the police. Don't go in, we may contaminate a crime scene." We are well trained by TV detectives. We stand.
"Mrs B, go and put the kettle on."
"What is the bag of jumble doing all over the hall floor?"
Miaow, miaow.
"What is Messe doing shut in there?"
We look at each other. "Did you call the police?"
"No, I thought you were."
"Wait, I'm going to look."
Cautiously we open the door a peep, jumping as the cat shoots out, with a turn of speed his footballing namesake would envy.
Slowly we push the door wider. On the floor is a poorly-stuffed jumble-clad dummy. A Donald Trump mask is topped with a yellow duster. The note stuck in its back with the paper knife reads: 'April Fool'.
"BOYS! DOWN HERE! NOW!"

Haiku

Woods of wild garlic

Bright stars shining in the shade

In the house they fade

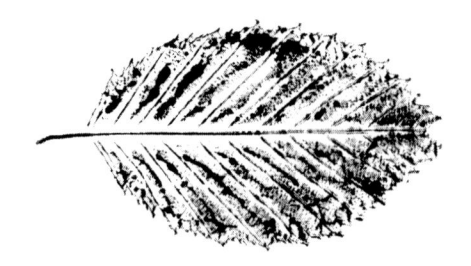

Gordon Hill

God Almighty!

Ah, someone at the door – Diana's answering it.
"Let me guess. You've come to save my soul? Great. Show me your proper ID. No! Not that silly business card, surely you've got a halo tucked into your pocket that you can expand and float above your head? No, and you expect me to take you seriously?"
"Your soul is no laughing matter."
"OK, so what's in it for you? I mean, like, how many souls do you have to save before you are allowed past St Peter?"
"Uh?"
"Salesmen like you have a commission structure, surely?"
"God has sent me to do his bidding. My reward is in the next life."
"Fine. Mark me up as saved in your database. I won't split on you if God calls me up to check. By the way, what's in it for God?"
"He sent his only son to save us."
"Why did he want to do that for a nasty lot like us? Anyway, it failed. All we did was nail him to a cross. I would have thought God would be a bit cheesed off about that and take revenge on us."
"But the point was that he sacrificed his son for us."
"It didn't work. Look at the world today."
"Ah, but it is our job to make sure it does work. Have faith."
"What? You look at the world today and say He can use you to fix

this mess? And what's all this faith business? I'm told I can move mountains with faith. I tried it once when I was out running on a rainy day in the Highlands and knackered with one more peak to go. It didn't move and God sent thunder and lightning as my reward for trying. Actually, I'd be quite happy now if I could use faith to stop the soup boiling over when I forget to keep an eye on it."
"You don't have enough faith."
"OK, where can I go to get it topped up?"
"It's not like that. You have to use faith properly."
"Right. Where can I get an instruction manual for faith?"
"It's right here in my hand – the Bible!"
"What? Hundreds of pages to dig through to get to how to move a mountain? There must be a quick guide, surely?"
"Join with us and all will become clear!"
"If I do, how long will it be before I can move a mountain?"
"Can we get off this mountain, please? I'm trying to save your soul!"
"What, using a book put together in around 500 AD by a load of clerics in smoke-filled committee rooms? Oh, I forgot, they didn't have tobacco. I wonder if they tried moving mountains in their lunch breaks?"
"Well, I do have tobacco, and need to calm my nerves. Can we resume sometime?"
"Yes of course. Just as soon as you've moved a mountain for me."

The Freezer

We're back at home after an excruciatingly boring hustings.

I say: "Even that dull uninteresting white slab of a freezer sitting quietly in the corner, even the old one in the garage, are more interesting than those politicians."

"A lot more," says Diana. "The new one isn't quiet. It's fussy too, doesn't like the cold garage. It has to occupy valuable space in the kitchen which now has to stay warmish even when we're away. All to save the world."

"Save the world?"

"Yes, Gordon, the old silent freezers and fridges, in fact all fridges and freezers then, were secretly plotting to destroy us so they could rule the world!"

"Are you nuts?"

"Well, perhaps I exaggerate slightly. When they wore out or were updated they were dismantled and took their revenge by releasing deadly CFC gas into the atmosphere."

"Oh, yes, I remember, the gas drilled a great big hole in the ozone layer and let ghastly UV (B) radiation through, damaging to many forms of life, even simple plankton in the sea. CFCs can stay there for up to a hundred years, so most of it is still there or heading there."

"Yes, Gordon, and each CFC molecule can destroy a hundred thousand ozone molecules!"

"So as soon as this was discovered, people stopped making CFCs?"

"Well, no, actually. Everyone needed time to adapt. Some countries said they needed more time and wouldn't agree or wanted big handouts to agree."

"What, Diana, delay, even if it meant serious damage, even the end of the world?"

"It's usually five years maximum to the next election. The destruction of the world, or, more accurately, human life on the world, takes a little longer. You don't want to act too soon, make it much more expensive to buy freezers and things and lose the next election, just to save the world."

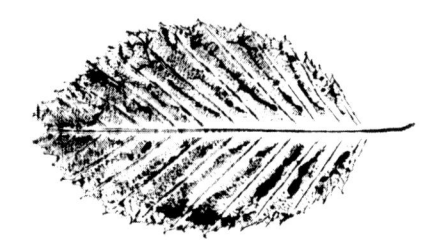

"Diana! That's really cynical. It can't be as bad as that!"

"Don't you believe it. Most of the old fossils who are powerful politicians won't be around to take the consequences of the delay. That's the way the world works. Short-termism always triumphs over good science. All you have to do is to convince people that there's a fix and it's fine."

"Oh! You are cynical, Diana. Why isn't it fine if the fix works?"

"Well, Gordon, the fix doesn't work if you don't do it, like you go on making CFCs for a few years and find you can't capture the CFCs when things are dismantled. The UV as a result of this will cause unusually high levels of mutation including amongst viruses and bacteria. This will lead to the risk of epidemics that might, probably will, wipe out the human race."

"Is that why no intelligent life has been discovered elsewhere in the universe? It always destroyed itself once it got fridges and freezers?"

"That's right, that freezer in the garage and its friends will be the cause of the end of the world."

"And I said that it was of no interest!"

That's It Then

Washing up's done and I can hear Diana sawing up a tree again. It's a warm day and it's taking her a while. But she's 84 and her heart isn't what it was. Let's go over with a glass of water - no tea left - and see what we can do, with my failing eyesight....oh, she's dripping sweat!

"You're overdoing it, Diana!"

"Perhaps. But we need lots of wood for the winter and you can't cut it now with your arthritis."

And I'm slow at getting potatoes in and other jobs. I know we're getting to the end but Diana fights on. We're the last two on earth. Nobody realised how fast society would disintegrate at the end. That worldwide epidemic of antibiotic resistant tuberculosis, unexpected collapse of a Greenland glacier releasing a huge hidden lake, major cities under water, revolutions, North Korea starting a nuclear war, the war spreading, failure of global food supplies, disintegration of society into starving mobs and roaming gangs, then.... Oh! Diana's stopped and is looking awful.

"Gordon, I need to lie down for a minute."

"There's a patch of grass just here."

She can't leave me. There's no one in the world left but us on this remote farm. "Don't look so worried, Gordon, I'll be fine; just give me a minute."

"I'll get a cushion and look for an aspirin. That'll help."

"Found, Diana, took a few minutes....."

Oh no, she's gone... no pulse, getting cold already. That's impossible, she can't do that.... No use crying but can't stop..... have to accept it....

That's it then, can't go on, it's all over for us and the human race. But it's a lovely evening so I'll sit quietly beside her with our last bottle of wine and our memories. At sunset a Permahappy pill will finish things for ever.

Christine Rae

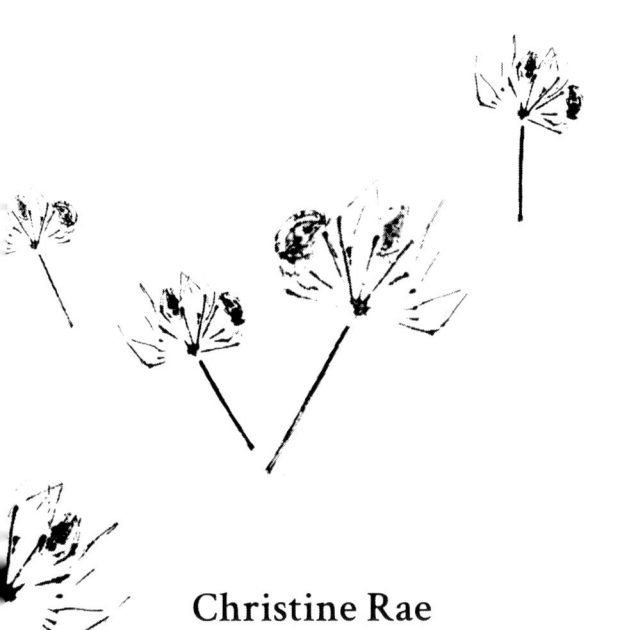

Strong Female

She was indomitable
Raised many children single-handed -
I knew of eight -
Fed them and cared for them
Till they were old enough to fly the nest
And branch out on their own.
Loving, confiding, giving pleasure to all:
Pullet - our self-tamed blackbird.

Heavenly Trine

Walking one early autumn morning
Rime-fringed grasses crisp under foot,
On my right the moon,
Crater-packed, still high in the western sky.
Eastward, the sun, a rising ball of fire
And I, ant-like,
Watching mesmerised from planet Earth.

Dragonfly

You
Are
A
Dragonfly
On shimmering wings
You lift me up
And show me beauty
When I falter
You give me strength.
Transforming all around you
You are
Beauty
Power
And
Peace

The Past Was Another Country

I was born on Christmas Eve 1945, a 'paid for' baby, before the NHS. My brother, born in 1948, was a 'King's baby', one of the first under the National Health. Very few people had cars and the roads were dusty so we often walked along green lanes, ancient trackways overhung by old trees and used by people to get from place to place over the centuries. I liked walking on them because the grass made my feet tickle.

Bath times were a tin bath in front of the fire, a warm nightie, and a soft featherbed. We had one with brass bedknobs which you could spin and play tunes on. For night-time there were potties in the bedrooms and during the day we used the privy. It had a cistern full of earth. You pulled a chain and the earth fell into a bucket. It was collected by a man who composted it and sold it to people as garden fertiliser.

There were no fridges. Food was kept cool in a brick or stone building attached to the house. There was no bottled milk; you took a jug to the nearest farm and had it filled. There was a thick layer of cream on top.

Christmas was fun except for two things - dishcloths, four - one for each aunt - dropped stitches and floods of tears from me! 'Thank you' letters drafted by mum, best handwriting and no crossings out because they were all teachers. If there were mistakes they were re-written: brother, two and a half years younger, got off with putting a kiss at the end.

School was tough. Teachers, all female, ruled classes of 40-45 children. No talking, no running and belting for mistakes.

Saturdays were great - exploring, tree-climbing, playing hopscotch and bursting tar bubbles.

Sunday was a downer. Dressed in good clothes, so that Mr and Mrs next door would see we weren't savages, we were frogmarched to church, and in the afternoon taken for a long walk to tire us out before another week of purgatory.

Creating Relations

The mighty Creator sat on his throne
He'd put all the stars in place
He'd separated light from dark
And sorted time and space.
He sent his angels to go and see
If they could find a spot
Which wasn't too cold and dreary
Nor terribly terribly hot.
They found a planet called Earth one day
That was absolutely right
So he made the sun for daylight
And the moon to shine at night.
He made the birds and animals
Two of each kind he made
And smiled as they enjoyed themselves
Playing in the woodland glade.
But there was something missing:
I've left out Man - dash me!
But what can I use to make them?
I know - I'll use streamside clay.
I'll mould them and I'll shape them
Until they are just right
And then I shall let them go free!
So children, we're all related
In a funny sort of way
For when God made us human
He gave us all feet of clay.

Convent Christmas

I am a little grey convent mouse
Living quietly in my cosy hole.
If I reveal some secrets
Does that turn me into a mole?
Well - on Christmas Day in the convent
There's an atmosphere of joy
And they celebrate the birthday
Of Mary's baby boy.
And while they are singing of Wise Men and shepherds
And angels with unfurled wings,
I've got to admit that my mind is fixed
On rather more secular things!
I've just been down to the kitchen
And things are doing fine,
The puddings are bubbling merrily
And they've opened the Blue Nun wine.
They always serve turkey sliced ready -
It saves arguments I suppose
For if everyone wanted a drumstick
Who'd be left with the parson's nose?
After lunch in the peace of her study
The Reverend Mother naps,
When some sisters are watching on telly
The tale of the singing von Trapps.
And when they all gather for Vespers
They all together pray,
That they may be spared next year to spend
Another happy Christmas Day.
And now that it's really a silent night
And the lights have gone out on the trees
I'm nipping off down to the kitchen
To finish that Stilton cheese!

Barry Bryan-Dixon

Tobacco Dock

Large ships, small ships, tall ships, in and out of docks on the Thames,
    Pleasure boats, rowing boats and other little craft:
Ships that are the lifeline to this great London City of mine.

Tobacco Dock is one such place for workmen to queue and wait:
    Uncles Johnny, Tommy, Fred and Burt to name a few.
Sometimes they needed twenty strong men, other times only eight.

In the docks, ships from exotic places and sailors with different faces,
    What wonderful stories each one might tell.
Where they have been, what they have seen, bet a tale they could tell.

Cranes looking like giraffe all along the water front moving gracefully,
    Lifting cargo from ships' holds.
Transfer to lorries stacking high, going on a journey as yet untold.

Many years later, walking by the Thames: large ships, smaller ships.
    Not so many visit our docks any more.
Pleasure boats, rowing boats criss-crossing up and down, or moored.

Not so many giraffe can be seen along the water front, and in between
 Not a ship or docker to be seen.
Tobacco Dock is closed down. Uncle Johnny finds a job in town.

No more ships from exotic places, or sailors with different faces,
 Tobacco Dock is boarded up, padlocked and chained.
A sad-looking sight never to be used as a dock again. Shame!

The rot is setting in. Planners want it used. Where do they begin?
 Then one day suggested some bright spark,
"I know we'll build yuppie flats and a beautiful themed outlet park."

It will bring employment to local people and money to local economy.
 The build had ended. The opening ceremony:
Flags were out, bands playing, the Mayor and dignitaries attending.

Yuppie flats, yuppie shops, locals could only window-shop.
 Bus route invented from City to East End.
Local people didn't gain much. When is it going to all end?

There's a scaled-down model ship in the dock just now,
 It looks magnificent from bow to stern.
Not the same as the real thing. No sailors with different faces.

The heart and spirit have been torn out of this wonderful place,
 Gone for ever never to return.
The local people and economy have no place. What a bloody disgrace!

Barry Bryan-Dixon

Wartime Childhood

Sirens, droning noises, clattering noises, whining noises, very loud bangs with a womph, or a sound like a plank of wood falling on the ground, flashing lights, big lights searching the sky. Being picked up by my Nan, Grandad, or some other member of the family, and carried from the house to another building every time all of these noises were heard. I had my own bed in there. The adults only had enough room to stand or sit. They would sing songs such as *You Are My Sunshine, Run Rabbit Run,* and *Knees Up Mother Brown.* They also recited nursery rhymes like *Humpty Dumpty, Mary Mary,* and *Sing A Song Of Sixpence.* As you have probably guessed by now, I am talking about the Second World War. What I have just described was almost a daily occurrence, I knew no other way of life until the war ended.

I was born in Hackney General Hospital in the East End of London in December 1941. My Mother and I were evacuated very soon after my birth to the West Country. A few weeks later my Grandad visited us both, and decided that we should return to Essex with him. He told my Mother that he and Nan would bring me up, while my Mother, who was still only sixteen, should carry on doing her fire-watch duties, hanging out with her friends and being a teenager. I didn't know that my Mother was my Mother until I was four years old. As far as I was concerned Nan and Grandad were my Mother and Father and I thought my Mother was my Aunt.

In spite of the war and its restrictions I had a brilliant childhood. We all did. I was, and still am, seen as the tenth child and the baby of the family. Brought up with my nine Uncles and Aunts - only my Aunt Mary and Uncle Arthur are still alive - I have a weird relationship with them. My Uncles and Aunts were my Brothers and Sisters, but of course when I was old enough I understood the difference, and paid them proper respect. Old as I am, I still call them Uncle and Aunt, but when we are talking about Nan and Grandad we refer to them as Mum and Dad.

Every morning Grandad and I would have porridge for breakfast. I would have sugar on mine and Grandad salt on his. Yuck! It was a ritual that I looked forward to every day.

I even used to help him sweep our chimney. We would push our huge oak dining table up to the fire place and sweep the chimney from under there, just in case of an air raid. When he finished sweeping the chimney, he always left the brush up there and asked me to go outside to see if the brush was out the chimney. He used to make me laugh by wriggling the brush about and pushing it up and down.

One day Nan was getting the washing line ready to hang the washing out, and Grandad asked me to go outside to look at the brush. I got to the back door. Nan started shouting at me which was something she never did. She ran towards me. The next thing I knew, Nan picked me up and threw me back into the kitchen. I landed in a heap on the floor at the back of the kitchen against the wall. I heard a clattering noise. Nan was still shouting. Our house had been strafed by a German fighter plane. It used Nan and me for target practice. As it turned out we were both O.K. I was not old enough to understand what had happened that day. All I know is I got lots and lots of cuddles. If only that old oak table could talk, it would have many a tale to tell.

At the bottom of our road was a field. My mates and I used to build dens in that field with some older boys. We dug an area of turf roughly six feet by four feet, put the turf to one side, then we dug down about eighteen inches or so, placing the earth on three sides of the hole. Then we would place pieces of timber or tree branches on top of the earth mounds. There were plenty of corrugated sheets around, so we used that for the roof and placed the turf on top of that. That was our den made. All we needed now was a fire to cook our bakeys (potatoes) on the fire. Just heaven to peel the charcoaled skin away to find white fluffy potato underneath, with the odd black finger print on it, well all over it to be correct. Many a very happy hour we spent in that field. We didn't know who owned it, but whoever he or she was: "thank you," it was appreciated.

Just down from the field was the River Chelmer. During the war we were not allowed down there because there was a battery of anti-aircraft guns along the river bank. That was where my future stepfather was based. I must have been about four when my mum took me down to the gun site to meet my new Dad. I didn't need a new Dad. Grandad was my Dad. Anyway this man frightened me. He was a giant of a man, six feet two inches tall. That was when I found out that Aunty Jean was my Mother, but I wasn't old enough to understand the situation.

Like a lot of families we took an American Serviceman into our house. His name was Jimmy Pyron. He was a bomb-loader on a ground crew with the US Bomber Command. I remember him sitting me on his knee and encouraging me to search in each of his pockets for sweets, chocolates and other goodies. We all loved him like one of the family. After the war we kept in touch, I was writing to his daughter until I joined the forces myself.

Carol Salsbury

Orphans

He sniffed the air – something was different, but he couldn't tell what. There was a dampness, certainly, but something else, a smell that seemed to be transformed in his brain to colours and textures – and taste. He hadn't realised until then how empty his belly was, but now he felt compelled to follow his nose, the browns and the greens, the soft wetness and the harsh sharpness beneath his feet, to see if food had somehow followed him to this alien place.

He was vaguely aware of his brothers, waiting behind him: he was the first to have stepped outside, the brave one. But now he ignored their uncertain shuffling – they would have to take care of themselves from now on. It was time to look after number one. He walked out into the unknown...

"I'm so glad we found them in time, goodness knows how long they'd have survived on their own. Look at them, poor wee things, let's get them inside and warmed up, then we can decide what to do for the best."

A box was located, lined with newspaper (heaven only knows where it came from, as reading the papers had never been something that took place in that household), and a hot water bottle, filled and wrapped in soft fleece, placed within. The tiny babies were gently laid on the improvised bed and covered over with warm blankets, while their rescuers tried to work out the best course of action.

"We'll phone Amy – she'll know what to do. And the hospital: should we take them there, d'you think? Or just phone them?"

"It's up to you, love. I know you'd rather take care of them yourself, if you can. But it's a lot to take on."

"Oh, but look at them, they're so tiny, and so cold, and they look as if they're starving. And they'll need some fluid too - they seem really dehydrated."

And so it was, at the beginning of October, the five brothers began their strange adventure. Little did they know that many others of their kind were not so lucky, had wandered, abandoned to their fate by parents drawn to ensure their own survival, and would most surely have frozen or starved to death.

He tried to remember his first memory of the warm sanctuary where he and his brothers had been raised. He recalled a sudden feeling of softness, smells so alien he felt he ought to be afraid, sounds that had no meaning to his young mind, and bright, bright lights. And yet there was only warmth, sustenance, and his brothers. He couldn't remember quite how they came to be there. He had felt sure he was all alone, but he was glad of the comfort of their closeness

Gradually, over the next few weeks, the brothers got stronger. At first, their benefactor had syringed warm water into their tiny mouths, before wrapping them up again in their cosy blankets, to sleep all huddled up with each other and with the ever-present hot water bottle.

Soon the syringes contained a thin meaty soup, which helped the brothers gain enough strength to take tentative mouthfuls of the food that miraculously appeared every day. It wasn't long before they were tucking in to platefuls of meat in between the many naps that their young bodies needed to grow.

There was one particular sound, always accompanied by the same identifying odour, that he came to recognise. Every day, he and his brothers were woken by this sound, and soon realised that it meant that it was time to have their bed changed, which he remembered fondly, for he loved the fresh clean smell of the new bedding. Sometimes the sound meant that he would be held aloft, often in very bright lights, and with more of the strange sounds all around. Sometimes it meant that he would be made to enter a warm, bubbly liquid, where he would be scrubbed before returning to the soft bed. He had come to realise that this one sound was a sort of communication, and that it was trying to be friendly. He resolved to return the friendliness – at least for a while.

The Refugees

Oh no – what's she brought back now? "Hi mum, I'm so glad to see you. Have you had a nice day?" *I bet you have, you traitor, and what exactly do you call this? Apart from something else to share your attention.*

"Hello, darling. I'll get your tea in a minute. Let me just settle our visitors in."

"But mum, I'm starving! And surely I come first." *And anyway, the 'visitors', whoever they are, smell disgusting. God only knows what they eat, to smell like that. Obviously nothing civilised.*

"Now, don't be so unkind, sweety. They're really lost and confused. How would you feel if you found yourself in a strange place, without your parents to feed and comfort you?"

"I don't care about them. This is my home, not theirs, and I think you should look after your own, before taking in waifs and strays!" *For goodness sake, woman, what next? I'll be having to give up my bed soon, and there won't be enough food to go round. I might just have to pack up and leave. That'd serve her right, if she got up one morning, and couldn't find me. That'd teach her.*

"Come on, just give me a minute. I'll be with you soon. Stop making such a fuss."

"But you've been out all day, and I've been waiting for you to come back, and I need..., well, I need you to look after me." *And I thought you'd always put me first, you horrid woman. Shows how wrong you can be. And she thinks she's being kindhearted? Just selfish, that's what she is. What about me? What about her own family? Don't we count anymore? Do we have to share her with those... those..., oh I don't know, but they look different, and they don't talk, and they SMELL.*

"Do you want to say hello to your new friends?"

"Do I have to? Oh, alright, if it'll make you happy." *Then perhaps you'll get me something to eat. The things I have to do to get some attention in this house.*

"Come on, they won't bite. They're just a bit frightened."

"Erm... Hello?..." *I bet they don't even speak my language. Why am I bothering?* "I said....HELLO!" *Haha, that got some reaction. Didn't expect them to curl up like that though.*

"Gently, darling, you've frightened them." *That WAS my intention, mother!*

"Come on, let's leave them alone for a while to settle in. I'll just give you your tea."

Hoo-bloomin'-ray, at last. It comes to something when a cat of my standing has to take second place to baby bloody hedgehogs!

Liberation

Oh, this smells good! I'm kind of tempted to go exploring with the others, but how do I know it's safe? At least here I know there'll be shelter and food... but - oh, it smells good! There's a vague memory, tickling the back of my brain, I've smelled this before, but it's so long ago I can't quite place it.

Where are they now? Oh, for goodness' sake, what are they doing? That can't be good for them, my feet are feeling cold and wet already, and I certainly don't feel like scrabbling around in the dirt – the dirt... it smells lovely. It smells of food, and... home?

Why would I be thinking about that? This is my home, this is where we've all been living together, where the food has been plentiful, the surroundings warm, and comfortable, the smells so different, sharp and clean.

I don't want to leave here – where are you going? I see they've managed to dig a hole between them, can't think why they're so desperate to get out, I like it here.

The smell... I can't stop thinking about it. Perhaps that's why they're all behaving so strangely, perhaps the smell is making them do things, perhaps it's a magic that turns you into – oh, I don't know.

They're leaving! They're all going off without me! What'll I do, what'll I do? I can't stay on my own, it doesn't feel right (or does it? Another tickle in my brain). Hey, guys, are you sure about this? Well they seem to be, they're not even sticking together, all going off exploring on their own. Okay, deep breath, here I go, follow the smell.

Bit of a squeeze getting through the gap they made, but if they could do it...

Oh WOW!

City Rap

Keep your head down, focus on the ground
Fix your face into a sad frown
Hurry hurry
Busy busy
Grey grey
City city
People
Times for friends are few, too much work to do
Always chasing after what is new
Hurry hurry
Busy busy
Grey grey
City city
People
Walk the dark street, never slow your feet
Listen to your frantic heartbeat
Hurry hurry
Busy busy
Grey grey
City city
People

Philip Hussey

New York, New York

"Oh no, I've forgotten my fags. Could I cadge one of yours, John?" Sitting on the new steel beam of the Empire State Building, Jeff had searched his pockets and realised with a sinking heart that he had forgotten his cigarettes.

He had been working as a steel erector for over six years during the New York skyscraper boom. The difference between his life here and that of his native rural Ireland could not have been more profound.

He glanced at the landscape below. No fear of heights: he lost all that whilst climbing trees in Donegal. Shuffling along the beam at break times was always a bit of a problem but he never had any fear of falling. Well, only once.

The hooter sounded and all the fag ends were flicked into the bottomless void.

I say just once, but that once was fatal. It happened six years ago. Jeff had just joined his work gang, mostly Irish but the foreman was from Lithuania. Where Lithuania was, Jeff didn't have a clue. They could hardly understand a word he said. The less they understood the angrier the Lithuanian got, so in the end the men just nodded their heads and got on with their work.

This day had started fine; it was a Monday, after a wet weekend.

The work on the previous Friday had been finished in a rush. The targets had been met but the checking had not been completed. The foreman shouted, but the men ganged up on him and were gone.

All thoughts of Friday were long forgotten; but not by the beam. The beam with only one bolt through; and that one bolt and nut not properly tightened. There were, of course, to be consequences.

The gang was split into two, with the majority working at a lower level, fixing angle irons to the main support beams.

John and Jeff were sent to the top of the building. The foreman had noticed the unsecured beam and gave specific instructions that the first job was to make it safe.

"Do ... you ... understand?" John and Jeff had nodded sagely.

According to Newton's laws of gravity, both a light and a heavy object, falling from a great height should hit the ground at the same time. The screwdriver, being more aerodynamic, hit the ground first, shattered, narrowly missing the tea boy who had been taken on only the week before.

The heavier object hit the ground a fraction of a second later and this time the consequences for the tea boy were not so fortunate.

Granny

"Oh! What's that funny noise?"

"Don't want to frighten you, Granny, but it looks like the lift's jammed."

"Well, we'll just have to sit tight and see what happens. There's no point in panicking and by-the-way, my name's Joan."

"If it's all the same to you, I'll call you Granny. I'm no good with names, see. My name's Kevin, but you can call me Kas."

"Kevin, there are only two of us stuck in this lift, surely you can remember 'Joan' for the next half an hour or so?"

"No, no, I don't mind if you call me Kas. In fact I prefer Kas to Kevin. How long do you think we'll be stuck like, as I've got an important meeting at four?"

"Kevin, you seem a bright boy; I'm sure you know a lot more about engines and machines than I do. However, I think we should know something within half an hour or so."

"No. It's just that you're old like and I thought you might have been stuck in a lift before. I hope you don't mind me saying this but you look like the sort of person who could have been stuck loads of times."

"That's very sweet of you, Kevin, but I'll let it pass. What's this important meeting you have at four o'clock? Perhaps you've got a job interview, although you don't look dressed for an interview. When I was your age, men going to interviews had to wear suits but nowadays anything seems to go. I blame the Americans. It was after the war; everything seemed to go to the dogs."

"I shouldn't really tell you this like but I'm bursting to tell someone. I feel a bit of a genius really but you won't like it and being a granny, you probably won't even understand. You see there's this guy who runs this massive haulage company, he's called Michael, Michael Thomas-Brown I think; can't stand people with double-barrelled names. Anyway, I was able to hack into their computer and plant a virus so that on every Tuesday they are unable to print any delivery tickets. My mate Dez who works in the office told his boss that I was a whiz with computers and would be able to sort out the problem. Knowing the problem I'll be able to fix it within an hour but I'll mess about for three or four hours. It's Friday today so I'll have it sorted by Saturday. I told him it would cost £500 cash. Clever eh? Money for old rope, there's one born every day. Hang on, the lift's moving, we should be out in a few minutes!"

"Not so quick Kas, I feel happy now about calling you Kas, because I definitely have the measure of you. You're right, Kas. The doors are opening, and the man you're about to meet is my son. Michael!"

Strange Meeting

I met my father coming towards me, on a country road. It all looked familiar but I couldn't quite remember how I got there.
"Dad, what are you doing here? You're dead."
"That's a fine way to greet your father, for as you can see I'm in the rudest of health." My father was dressed in his usual way; Wellington boots and baggy trousers held up with binder twine. I was in my early sixties and my father looked less than thirty. Back at the farm I was probably asleep in a cot.

A strange meeting indeed; it took several evenings on my own and several nights' sleep to work it out. When I returned home to my wife, the usual greeting of "How was your day?" left me momentarily stumped. "Oh, tiring, I think I'll have a bath and an early night."

I studied Theoretical Physics at university; it's funny how thoughts come to one soaking in the bath; my PhD thesis was based on trying to resolve the contradictions in the theory of the Space-Time Continuum. There was a knotty problem at the time; a shift of half a degree in the tilt of the Earth would cause significant issues. What could possibly have caused a momentary shift such that after a few minutes, everything reverted to normal?

Scouring the internet, I found that Pakistan had exploded a nuclear device two hours before my strange meeting. The device was a hydrogen bomb and an explosion of this magnitude would certainly have resulted in a half of a degree shift. Using the coordinates of the explosion I plotted the time distortion. The time-shift I calculated to be sixty years, fifty nine days, nine hours and twenty minutes plus or minus ten minutes.

In my childhood I cannot remember my father talking about this strange meeting. He probably thought that he had imagined it. How could he have explained meeting his sixty-year-old son on his way back from work when the same son was asleep in a cot?

This is the first time I have dared relate this story and I do it now only as fiction. My old professor, Professor Hope, would have smiled gently and said "Philip, you always had a fertile imagination."

Tin Can

Dave had always dreamt of becoming an astronaut. Even now he didn't regret his decision, even though events were starting to take a turn for the worst. He smiled at this English turn of phrase; in reality, things could hardly get any worse. He sat back in his seat and remarked absentmindedly to his colleague, "What do we do now?"

"Ne ponimayu, ne ponimayu."

The long hours passed. He would now have a long time to think. Dave thought back to his early years. It was the lunar module *Eagle*, landing on the Moon, that first sparked his interest. Back in 1969 he was still a child and his dad had allowed him to stay up late. Neil Armstrong was walking on the Moon. "I want to be an astronaut when I grow up."

"I wouldn't get too carried away son, you'd be better driving a truck like your Pa."

Dave was not easily put off; he studied maths and the sciences and eventually took a degree in astro-physics at MIT.

Yuri brought him back to the present. "Ne ponimayu, ne ponimayu."

What Yuri didn't understand, Dave wasn't sure. "If it's any help, I don't understand either." Conversations were usually short between the two of them, normally restricted to the technical information required to fly the spacecraft.

Another long period of silence ensued. After training as a test pilot with the American Air Force, Dave was recruited into the Astronaut Programme. He thought however that his dream would fail at the last hurdle: the Shuttle series had ground to a halt and America seemed to have lost interest in space travel. Trump's short term as president hadn't helped. 'Shooting from the hip' as usual, he had managed to plunge the world into crises. Dave saw a chance, though, and took a crash course in Russian. Putin wanted to humiliate America and was offering an opportunity for an American astronaut to travel in its latest space mission; Dave was the obvious candidate. He put Trump to the back of his mind and left for Russia two months later. Another three weeks and he was climbing aboard the Soyuz spacecraft. He was surprised that it was still a Soyuz rocket, for he had been told that they would be conducting the inaugural flight of Russia's new rocket, currently unnamed. He had a worrying feeling but Yuri did not seem unduly concerned.

They were orbiting the Moon before the main task of their mission and the retro-rockets had been fired. They were expecting a short burst to take them out of the first orbit and into a second. The rocket firing seemed to go on forever; for the first time Yuri was looking worried.

"Ground control, what's happening?" A shaky voice replied, "Don't worry, we will resolve the problem and contact you in one hour."

That was twenty eight days ago. Yuri had obeyed the command and taken his pill. He was still in his seat quietly decomposing. Dave had put on his spacesuit and was oblivious to the smell. Yuri's dying meant that the air supply could last up to a month. All contact had been lost. Not for the first time he sang "Sitting in a tin can far above the world…"

Beverley Vaux

The Shepherdess

The alarm rings at two o'clock,
Quickly turn to switch it off
Silently slip out of bed
Dress and put on overalls.

Out into the cold night air
To the lambing sheds I go.
This is the time I love best
Stillness, silence, all alone.

Breathless sky is filled with stars
Billion diamonds twinkling bright
Wide arc of the Milky Way
Swinging clear to eternity.

Beverley Vaux

Into the shed: smell of sheep
Warm and rustling; murmurings
Of ewes comforting their lambs
Suckling and softly bleating.

Quietly turn on the light
Scan the shed for new life signs:
Then I see a sheep straining
Has she been in labour long?

Quickly I put on my gloves,
Grab my crook and can of dye.
She leaps up as I arrive
Drops her lamb and runs away.

Sheep shoots past, I squirt the can.
"Got you!" I say to myself,
Lift the lamb by its fore-legs
Put it in a separate pen.

Then I go back for the ewe.
Fling my crook to grab her neck,
Another sheep jumps at me
Sends me crashing to the ground.

Sheep trample all over me.
When I stagger to my feet
Glad I marked her when I could,
I prepare to try again.

Finally I corner her,
Grab her by the scruff of neck,
Leap astride her, hanging on
Frog-march her from the pen.

Reunited with her lamb
The ewe calms and starts to lick.
When I have a second feel
There seems to be another!

Her second lamb will appear
In its own good time I think.
So I leave them on their own
To get to know each other.

All now quietly calm and warm.
Softly I turn off the light
Out into the grey of dawn
Exhausted but satisfied.

Quietly creep into the house,
Change and slip between the sheets,
Snuggle down; there comes a shriek
"Take away those icy feet!"

Beverley Vaux

The Jewelled Way:
A Walk near Gatehouse of Fleet

Just an ordinary day; just an ordinary walk. But brilliant sun, crystal air and a gentle breeze gave a magic to the day. Although this was one of our usual walks, the heady scent of the sapphire bluebells and ruby soldiers' buttons made us more aware of everything around us. Strolling on, I glimpsed a path, unnoticed before - untrodden, overgrown with grass; leading upwards, steeply upwards.

Whistling for the dog, we took that way and plunged into a different universe. Like entering a vast cathedral, jade light filtered through the canopy far above us. Walking silently now, footsteps cushioned by emerald moss and amber needles, reverently through the gigantic sacred nave, seemingly endless as we climbed. Scampering over occasional fallen trunks, then onwards, still upwards in this deep green world; swimming through a flooded ruin, engulfed and abandoned. Was that a muffled, slowly tolling bell, moved by the gentle rocking of the tide or just the soughing of the wind in the branches high above? No sound of birds, no other noise of any kind, just a silent, numinous space with occasional emerald glints of sunlight through the boughs.

Then, suddenly, out in the open, heathery hills before us and the path leading on, a carpet of amethyst: dog violets - yellow striped tongues hanging out, panting in the sun. On and on, never have I seen such a myriad of violets threaded through with tiny lady's-mantle, diamonds of dew, half hidden among her frilly leaves; little brown birds flitting and twittering in the trees, chiffchaffs calling and in the distance on the hill, a cuckoo sounding his summer song.

Where is the path now? Is this the end, a former turning bay? No, there is a narrow rocky trail to the right, deer or human, I do not know, but follow it anyway. This is a scramble over great granite rocks among small spruce, larch and heather to the top but the view is still obscured. Could these rocks hide the lead and Galloway gold and silver, mined at Wanlockhead, Pibble and the Garyhorn? The precious Scottish metals from which the magnificent Michael Lloyd Mace was made. Surely they could be hidden here too?

Then plunging steeply down, in single file, between imperial topaz buttercups, gleaming stitchwort, star-of-Bethlehem and lapis speedwell, with distant glimpses of a golden waving tail. Out on to the wide track again and diving back into our solemn underwater forest world of deep opalescent silence, sacred and mysterious. Then the great west doors are open before us onto the everyday world.

Will that hidden way be there again with its treasure house of gems or were we the only ones permitted to venture into this enchanted land?

Savonarola

So this is how it ends.

Hanging from a tree.

The all-consuming fire burns bright beneath

My friends on either side already dead,

Their bodies flaming as I climb the gibbet steps.

What's that you ask? How do I feel?

"The Lord has suffered as much for me."

My whole life has been a quest

To restore church and state to holiness and purity,

Beverley Vaux

To mortify my flesh and cleanse my soul.
My daily practice: rise at dawn,
Wash with cold water, scourge my body,
Put on the hair belt next my skin
Under my simple friar's robes.
I have seen the church corrupted:
Pope Alexander's love of wealth and luxury,
This age of enlightenment, started with good intent,
Turn to a world of greed, gambling, evil and profanity.
The Lord made me Prior of San Marco's Convent,
Gave me dominion over the whole State.
We set up a democratic Republic:
Florence, the New Jerusalem!
No more exploitation of the poor,
Youth committed to assist
Cleansing bonfires of the vanities here,
Right beneath my feet.
They even offered me a Cardinal's red hat.
I just want purification – a hat of righteous blood.
How have I been repaid? Excommunication!
My prophecies and visions vilified,
Tortured and now hanged and burnt.
The Lord will have his revenge.
It is an honour so to die.
Yes indeed! "The Lord has suffered as much for me."

The Contributors

Stella Cruickshank was born in Bideford in Devon. She trained and worked as a nurse at St Bartholomews, London. After she married, she and her husband lived in Cornwall, Sussex, the Highlands and Sweden. They moved to the Glenkens four years ago. Before joining the Glenkens Writers' Group Stella had never written. Her poem, 'The Book Festival' was published in the *Herald* at the beginning of this year's Edinburgh International Book Festival.

Merryn Fergusson was brought up mainly in Cornwall, Malaya and Germany. Merryn and her husband Alex farmed in South Ayrshire until 1999 when they moved to the Glenkens. Merryn wrote *What is Wrong with ME* after their youngest son recovered from severe ME, during which he missed three years of school. Her second book, *Vertigo and the Vagus Nerve*, explores physiotherapy in dizziness and labyrinthitis. She has recently finished a novel based on her French grandfather who disappeared shortly after WW1.

Roger Adams explains why he writes: "It's about walking, witnessing lives, accepting help. Sweltering endless Judean wilderness, I become so grateful to the Arab on his tractor. Rain, a wet climb, miles to Lochgoilhead until, 'what you need', said the forester, 'is a lift'. Dhaka, Bangladesh, dawn, a miserable passenger; disembarking the launch, I witness Christa, waving." Roger is a sociologist (BSc. MA, M.Phil), watches Al Jazeera TV, always wants to know what is happening, where, look at his maps and think, "where next?"

The Contributors

Ann Maxwell's entire life has been connected with agriculture in some form. She was born and brought up in Norfolk, except for three years when she was evacuated to the Lake District. In 1956, having completed a foundation Art course, Ann went as an assistant matron and art teacher to a girls' school in Rhodesia. She married John and raised her oldest three children in Nyasaland. They had another child when they moved to farm in the Glenkens in 1964.

Margaret Pringle was born in Edinburgh. In 1945 she joined the Land Army working on a dairy farm near Stranraer. After three years at West of Scotland Agricultural College, she taught at an agricultural college for girls in Harrismith, South Africa. Margaret was appointed a field officer by Crown Agents to oversee animal husbandry in Tanganyika for another three years and then she stayed in South Africa where she raised her family. Margaret moved to the Glenkens in 1993.

Wendy Davis moved to New Galloway in 1994 from the Manchester area where she was senior lecturer in the university's Education Department. Originally a P.E. teacher, she moved into teacher training after the births of her two sons. She developed an Arts and the Community degree with over 200 student placements in the disadvantaged communities of the region. In 2001 she joined the newly-formed GCAT, continuing to work with them for several years. Her interests include gardening, painting, spinning, weaving, writing and travelling.

Gordon Hill graduated in Physics at Edinburgh University in 1967. Amongst other things he has developed radio transmitters and other instrumentation to track animals and monitor people's heart and brain activity. Since moving to New Galloway he has worked on local footpath developments and is a Sustrans Ranger for Route 7. He is currently writing two novels and enjoying trail-running.

Barry Bryan-Dixon was born in the East End of London and brought up and educated in Essex. He signed on in the Royal Army Medical Corps for 22 years and retired from the forces in 1981. He worked as a bus driver for 28 years and retired to New Galloway in 2013. He now volunteers for Dumfries Hard of Hearing Group.

Christine Rae was born in Somerset and came to South West Scotland in 1955, aged five. She attended Kippford Primary School. Her family moved to Dalry in 1960 and, once she had trained as a speech therapist, Christine worked in Galloway. For many years Christine produced plays and performed in the local pantomimes. She inherited her love of words from her father who used to make up bedtime stories so that she would go to sleep happy.

The Contributors

Carol Salsbury is a retired teacher. She moved to the Glenkens 20 years ago to escape the stresses of city life and to be closer to nature. She gardens for wildlife and spent the winter rearing orphaned hedgehogs. Another of her passions is singing, and Carol belongs to two choirs as well as performing in an *a cappella* folk duo. She is enjoying the opportunity to write about the things closest to her heart.

Born in the last century, **Philip Hussey** studied chemistry, which turned out to be a mistake. He has worked for a company ethically disposing of toxic waste, as a pollution control officer and is now selling concrete products - so big in waste, sewage and now concrete. When he tells people this, their eyes glaze over. With this publication he can now say he's a writer with a published book; no more glazed eyes, well fewer anyway! Proud father of four children.

Beverley Vaux was born in Kent and spent her childhood in Rio de Janeiro. She came to school in England where reading and writing were her most important companions. Life then rather got in the way: secretarial college, working, marriage and children, charity work, farming and running a self-catering business. She is now enjoying writing in retirement.